A Palm Tree
On The
Beach

FACES
AND
PLACES

CUBA

BY KATHRYN STEVENS

THE CHILD'S WORLD®, INC.

COVER PHOTO

A young Cuban girl.
©Christophe Loviny/CORBIS

Published in the United States of America by The Child's World®, Inc.
PO Box 326
Chanhassen, MN 55317-0326
800-599-READ
www.childsworld.com

Project Manager James R. Rothaus/James R. Rothaus & Associates
Designer Robert E. Bonaker/R. E. Bonaker & Associates
Contributors Mary Berendes, Dawn M. Dionne, Katherine Stevenson, Ph.D., Red Line Editorial

Library of Congress Cataloging-in-Publication Data
Stevens, Kathryn, 1954–
Cuba / by Kathryn Stevens.
p. cm.
Includes index.
ISBN 1-56766-906-9 (lib. bdg. : alk. paper)
1. Cuba—Juvenile Literature.
[1. Cuba]
I. Title.
F1758.5 .S74 2001
972.91—dc21

Table
of
Contents

Earth's largest land areas are called **continents**. Just southeast of the continent of North America is a group of islands known as the West Indies. These islands lie at the northern edge of the Caribbean Sea. The largest island, Cuba, sits in the entrance to the Gulf of Mexico.

Western Hemisphere

Eastern Hemisphere

Cuba (white) and U.S.A. (green) are both in the west

The islands of Jamaica and the Bahamas are also in the West Indies. So is Hispaniola, home to Haiti and the Dominican Republic. To Cuba's north is Florida, in the United States. To the west is Mexico's Yucatan region.

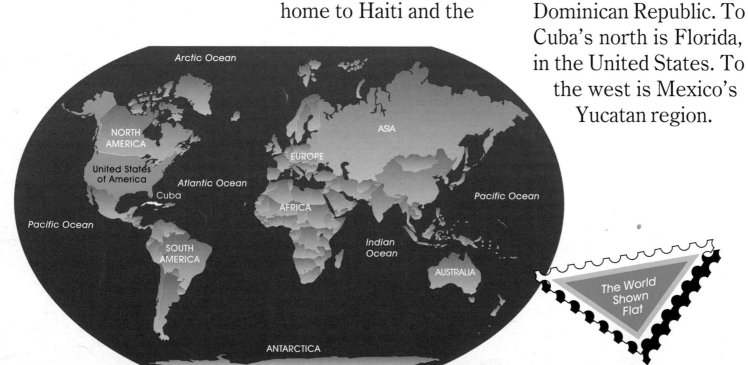

Arctic Ocean

NORTH AMERICA

United States of America

Atlantic Ocean

Cuba

ASIA

EUROPE

Pacific Ocean

Pacific Ocean

AFRICA

SOUTH AMERICA

Indian Ocean

AUSTRALIA

ANTARCTICA

The World Shown Flat

6

Close-Up
Of
Cuba

Gulf of Mexico

UNITED STATES
(FLORIDA)

Atlantic Ocean

BAHAMAS

CUBA

MEXICO

HAITI

JAMAICA

HONDURAS

Caribbean Sea

NICARAGUA

The Beach At Varadero

Havana Bay • Varadero

• Pinar del Rio

Cuban Landscape Near Pinar Del Rio

©Robert van der Hilst/CORBIS

Cuba's main island is surrounded by about 1,600 small islands. Cuba has some mountains, but most of the country is flat or rolling. The land is good for growing crops. Beautiful beaches, scenic shorelines, and coral reefs lie along the seacoast. The coast's many bays provide **harbors** where ships can land. Cuba's biggest harbor is Havana Bay, on the northwest coast.

Apartment Houses Overlooking Havana Bay

©Jeremy Horner/CORBIS

Cuba's **tropical** weather is generally warm and moist. The rainy season lasts from about May to October. The rest of the year is drier. The combination of good soil and plentiful rain is good for farming. Occasionally the island is hit by a **hurricane**, a tropical storm that can cause terrible damage from high winds and rains.

The Face Of A Cuban Crocodile

©Tom Brakefield/CORBIS

Cuba's plant life reflects its tropical climate. Thousands of types of plants grow on the island. Some of them grow nowhere else on Earth. At one time nearly half of the island was forested, but most of the forests have been cut down. Some areas, especially in the east, are still wooded. Palms are the most common trees, with over 30 different types. Other common trees in Cuba are cedar, mahogany, ebony, rosewood, and citrus.

A Forest Near Havana

©Christophe Loviny/CORBIS

Birds are plentiful—in fact, Cuba has over 300 different kinds. They include beautiful parrots, parakeets, hummingbirds, and flamingos. The island has many bats, too. The only native land mammals are the *hutia,* or cane rat, and the rare *solenodon,* a large, rat-like insect-eater. Cuba has tortoises, crocodiles, and iguanas. It also has snakes called Cuban boas that can grow to 12 or 13 feet long!

A Cane Rat In A Sugarcane Field

Statue Of Christopher Columbus In Cárdenas

★Havana •Cárdenas

©Eye Ubiquitous/CORBIS

Long Ago

Cuba's first people, the Ciboney, sailed from South America at least 3,000 years ago. Later, the Arawak and then the Taínos arrived. When Spanish explorer Christopher Columbus reached Cuba in 1492, over 100,000 native people already lived there.

Columbus thought he had reached faraway Asia and claimed the area for Spain. More Spanish people came, seeking gold and riches. During the 1500s, they forced the native Indians to work in mines or on farms. Conditions were so harsh that almost all the Native Americans died.

Even after the gold was gone, Spain fought to keep Cuba. Its location was important for ships sailing between Spain and the New World. In the 1600s to 1800s, the Spanish brought thousands of slaves from Africa to work in Cuba's mines and sugarcane fields. After winning the Spanish-American War in 1898, the United States ruled Cuba until 1902. The two countries maintained a close relationship for many years.

Sailing Ships In Havana Bay

Cuba Today

Today Cuba's leader is Fidel Castro (fee-DEL KAS-troh), who overthrew the previous ruler in 1959. Castro's government took control of almost all of Cuba's businesses, including some owned by Americans.

Hundreds of thousands of people left Cuba. Many of them were wealthy people who had lost their property. Today one million ex-Cubans live in the United States. Some still hope to return to the island and see Castro removed from power.

After Castro's **revolution**, Cuba and the United States were no longer on good terms. Instead, Cuba developed a close relationship with the **Soviet Union**, which bought Cuban products and provided aid. At times great tension existed between the three nations. Since the Soviet Union collapsed in 1991, Cuba has faced serious financial trouble. Shortages of food and other supplies are still a major problem.

©Wally McNamee/CORBIS

Fidel Castro Giving A Speech In Havana

★Havana

Capitol Building
In Havana

A Farm Laborer

★Havana

©Arne Hodalic/CORBIS

Cuban Soldiers Standing At Attention In Havana

©David & Peter Turnley/CORBIS

Cuba's people come from several different backgrounds. Most are descended, at least in part, from the Spanish. About one tenth are descended from the Africans that were brought to Cuba as slaves. Many people have mixed backgrounds because of intermarriage between the different groups.

A Worker In A Sugarcane Field Taking A Break

©Richard Powers/CORBIS

Catholicism, brought to Cuba by the Spanish, was once the island's most common religion. It has not been practiced as widely since Castro's revolution. Many Cubans no longer practice any religion. Others follow a religion called Santería (sahn-teh-REE-ah). Santería is a mixture of Catholicism and beliefs the early slaves brought from Africa.

City Life And Country Life

People Traveling On Cars And Bicycles In Cárdenas

©Kevin Fleming/CORBIS

About three-quarters of Cuba's people live in cities. Over 2 million live in Havana, the largest city. Gas is expensive, and few city dwellers drive cars. Instead, they rely more on bicycles. Most city dwellers live in apartments. Many buildings are in poor condition because money and building materials are in short supply.

Farmers Plowing A Field In Vinales

©Tom Bean/CORBIS

The rest of the people live in small villages or on farms in Cuba's **rural** areas. The gasoline shortage means that country dwellers also rely on bicycles. Many have even gone back to using horse-drawn wagons and ox-drawn plows. People in the country often live in simple homes, some with **thatched** grass roofs.

18

©Jeremy Horner/CORBIS

Havana
Cárdenas
Viñales

Buildings In
Central
Havana

Schoolgirls In
Uniform In
Vinales

★Havana
• Vinales

Books For Sale In Havana

©Jan Butchofsky-Houser/CORBIS

At 6 years old, Cuban children begin attending grade school. There they study subjects such as reading and math. After grade school many go on to middle school. Some later go to high schools and universities. All schooling is free. Before Castro's revolution, many Cubans could not read or write. Now almost everyone can read and write.

Planning A Fashion Collection At A Modeling School In Havana

©Arne Hodalic/CORBIS

Because of the long time Cuba spent under Spanish control, Cubans speak the Spanish language. Many of the Spanish who settled Cuba came from southern Spain. They pronounced words somewhat differently from people elsewhere in Spain. Cuban Spanish still sounds different from the kind of Spanish spoken in most of Spain.

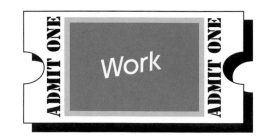

Work

For many years, Cuba's businesses and jobs were almost all controlled by the government. In the past few years, the government has allowed more people to own their own businesses and work for themselves. Many Cubans still cannot find good jobs, however.

About one-fifth of Cuba's workers are farmers. Cuba's largest crop is sugar, and the next largest is tobacco. Farmers also raise cattle, rice, coffee, fruits, and vegetables such as corn, beans, and carrots. Some people work in fishing. Others work as miners to remove copper and nickel from underground.

City dwellers work in a variety of jobs, including in businesses and factories. Some work at hotels and restaurants that serve visiting **tourists**. Because of differences between their two countries, Americans seldom visit Cuba. Instead, Cuba's tourists come from Canada, Europe, Latin America, and elsewhere. Tourism is encouraged because it brings much-needed money into the country.

©Richard Bickel/CORBIS

Tobacco Farmers In The Vinales Valley

Pinar del Rio • Vinales

Sugarcane Harvester In Pinar Del Rio

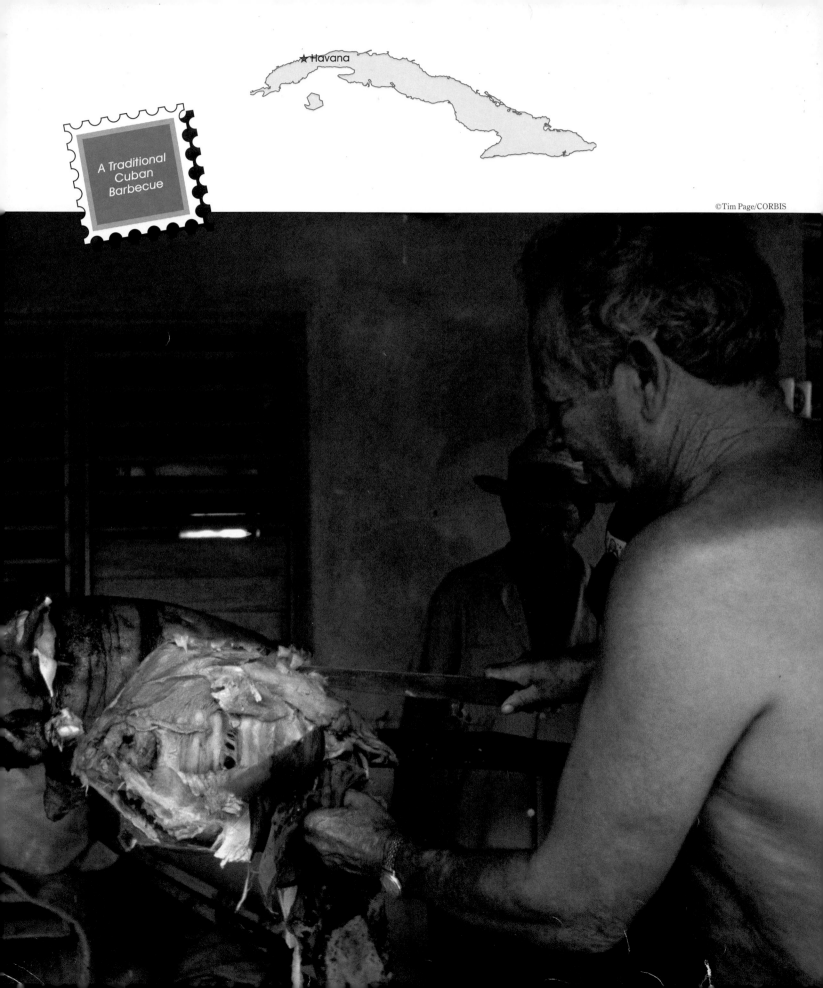

A Traditional
Cuban
Barbecue

★Havana

©Tim Page/CORBIS

Food

Cuba cannot grow all of the food it needs, so it must buy some from other countries. Food shortages have been common, especially since the Soviet Union collapsed. Use of many foods in Cuba is limited, or **rationed**. Many people cannot afford foods they would like to eat. Rice is eaten at every meal and is often served with black beans to make an inexpensive but tasty dish. Many people grow their own vegetables to add food to their tables.

Cuban foods reflect a mixture of cooking styles, including Spanish and African. *Ajiaco* (ah-HYAH-koh) is a stew made with meat and vegetables. *Arroz con pollo* (ah-ROHS kon POH-yoh) is a flavorful dish of chicken and rice.

Fruits are popular in Cuba, including juicy mangoes, grapefruit, pineapples, and bananas. Banana-like plantains (plan-TANES) are served in many different ways, including sliced and fried.

A Sandwich Station During A Cuban Food Crisis

©Richard Bickel/CORBIS

Pastimes and Holidays

Music and dance are popular in Cuba—especially drum-filled dancing music such as the cha-cha-cha, rumba, and mambo. Sports such as basketball, volleyball, and boxing are popular, too. Baseball is the Cuban people's favorite sport. Cuba's baseball players are respected around the world. The country's team won the gold medal at the 1996 Olympic Games. In the fast-moving game of jai alai (HY LY), players throw and catch a ball using curved baskets. Board games such as chess and dominoes are also popular.

Cuba's holidays celebrate important historical events. Liberation Day (January 1) marks Castro's rise to power in 1959. May Day (May 1) is International Workers' Day. Rebellion Day (July 26) marks the start of Castro's revolution in 1953. Cubans celebrate these holidays with parties, carnivals, parades, and political speeches. In 1997, the government once again permitted people to celebrate Christmas, which had been banned since the revolution.

Right now Cuba and the United States do not have a very friendly relationship, so few Americans travel there. But someday the two countries hope to get along better. Then perhaps you will be able to visit the island to enjoy its beautiful scenery, friendly people, and fascinating culture.

A Military May Day Parade In Havana

©Francoise de Mulder/CORBIS

A Baseball
Player In
Pinar Del Rio

Area
Including smaller islands, about 44,000 square miles (114,000 square kilometers)—about as big as Ohio.

Population
About 11 million people—about the same population as Ohio.

Capital City
Havana.

Other Important Cities
Santiago de Cuba, Camagüey, Holguín, Guantánamo, and Santa Clara.

Money
The Cuban peso (PAY-soh), made up of 100 centavos.

National Flag
A flag with two white stripes, three blue stripes, and a red triangle with a white star. The white stripes stand for pure ideas, and the blue stripes represent the blue ocean. The red stands for the blood of those who fought for Cuba.

National Song
"La Bayamesa," or "The Bayamo Song."

National Sport
Baseball.

Official Name
The Republic of Cuba.

Head of Government and Head of State
The president.

SO NEAR AND YET SO FOREIGN

90 Miles from Key West

A Cuban Travel Poster From The 1940s

VISIT CUBA

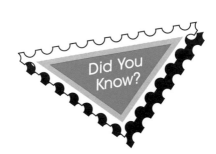

Before Cuban slavery was outlawed in the 1880s, slaves in the sugarcane fields usually died after only a few years because the work was so hard. When the slaves died, the owners simply brought in more.

In 1898 American soldiers, including soldiers on horseback called the "Rough Riders," helped defeat the Spanish in Cuba. The Rough Riders' leader was Theodore Roosevelt, who later became the president of the United States.

Unhappy with their life in Cuba, many people have tried to escape to the United States, setting sail in small boats or even homemade rafts. Many have died trying to make this dangerous voyage.

Despite Cuba's small size, it contains more than 10 percent of the world's known supply of nickel. Nickel has been one of Cuba's most important products to sell overseas.

Cuba is home to the world's smallest bird (the Cuban bee hummingbird) and the world's smallest frog (the banana frog).

	CUBAN SPANISH	HOW TO SAY IT
Hello	hola	OH–lah
Good Day	buenos días	BWAY–nos DEE–ahs
Good-bye	adiós	ah–dee–OSE
Please	por favor	por fah–VOR
Thank You	gracias	GRAH–see–ahs
One	uno	OO–no
Two	dos	DOHS
Three	tres	TRACE
No	no	NOH
Yes	sí	SEE
Cuba	Cuba	KOO–bah

continents (KON-tih-nents)
Earth's continents are huge land masses surrounded mostly by water. Cuba lies just southeast of the continent of North America.

harbors (HAR-berz)
Harbors are protected places along a coastline where ships can land safely. Cuba's coastline has many natural harbors.

hurricane (HUR-rih-kane)
A hurricane is a violent storm that hits some ocean areas with strong winds and lots of rain. Cuba sometimes experiences hurricanes.

rationed (RASH-und)
When something is rationed, it is given out only in limited amounts. In Cuba today, many foods and other scarce items are rationed.

revolution (rev-uh-LOO-shun)
A revolution is a violent uprising that changes a country's government. Cuban leader Fidel Castro came to power through a revolution.

rural (RUR-ull)
Rural areas are places out in the countryside, away from cities. Many people who live in Cuba's rural areas are poor.

Soviet Union (SOH-vee-et YOON-yun)
The Soviet Union was a country made up of Russia and nearby parts of eastern Europe and northern Asia. The Soviet Union had a communist government and was a major world power until it split apart into smaller countries in 1991.

thatched (THATCHT)
Thatched roofs are made of carefully stacked grass or straw. Some homes in the Cuban countryside have thatched roofs.

tourists (TOOR-ists)
Tourists are people who travel to a place to sightsee and visit. Cuba encourages visits by tourists.

tropical (TROP-ih-kull)
Tropical places have weather that is warm and moist all year. Cuba is a tropical country.

Index

Web Sites

Learn more about Cuba:
http://cubaweb.cu/Cub_ing/index.asp
http://www.latinworld.com/countries/cuba
http://library.thinkquest.org/18355/
http://www.state.gov/www/regions/wha/cuba/
http://www.lonelyplanet.com/destinations/caribbean/cuba/

Learn how to make some Cuban foods:
http://www.foodtv.com/cuisine/cubarecipes/0,3680,,00.html

Learn how to say more words in Spanish:
http://www.travlang.com/languages/
(Then be sure to click on the word "Spanish.")

Read a short biography of Fidel Castro:
http://www.cnn.com/resources/newsmakers/world/namerica/castro.html